Bernice Hurst

griddling

simple and delicious easy-to-make recipes

This is a Parragon Book
This edition published in 2005

Parragon
Queen Street House
4 Queen Street
Bath BA1 1HE, UK

ISBN: 1-40546-227-2

Printed in China

Produced by
THE BRIDGEWATER BOOK COMPANY LTD

Photography Trevor Leak
Home Economist Marianne Lamb

Cover Photography Calvey Taylor-Haw
Home Economist Ruth Pollock

NOTES FOR THE READER

- The nutritional information boxes show measurements calculated per portion of food.

- This book uses both metric and imperial measurements. Follow the same units of measurement throughout; do not mix metric and imperial.

- All spoon measurements are level: teaspoons are assumed to be 5 ml, and tablespoons are assumed to be 15 ml.

- Unless otherwise stated, milk is assumed to be low fat, eggs and individual vegetables such as potatoes are medium, and pepper is freshly ground black pepper.

- Recipes using raw or very lightly cooked eggs should be avoided by infants, the elderly, pregnant women, convalescents, and anyone suffering from an illness.

- Optional ingredients, variations or serving suggestions have not been included in the calculations.

- The times given are an approximate guide only. Preparation times differ according to the techniques used by different people and the cooking times vary as a result of the type of oven used.

contents

introduction

Griddling is an age-old method of cooking that has recently enjoyed a resurgence in popularity as a quick and easy way of creating attractive and delicious dishes. It is ideal for entertaining and for making nibbles. If you want to focus on the flavour of just one or two excellent ingredients, then this is one of the best methods to use. While any sauces have to be prepared separately rather than used to cook the main ingredients, the opportunity to use marinades and contrasting dressings or accompaniments more than compensates for this.

Some planning is required: for example, some skewers will be too long, those with handles may not fit in your pan, and when using wooden sticks, you should first soak them in water for half an hour to prevent burning. Toothpicks make excellent skewers for griddled miniature canapés, as do sprigs of rosemary or lemon grass.

lemon-grilled salmon
page 16

seared duck breast
page 52

The very essence of the griddling method is to create charred and blackened surfaces to the food you are preparing. Successful griddling entails heating the pan until it is very, very hot and then searing the surface of the food you are cooking over as high a heat as it can stand. Be aware that griddling can be a smokey process, so we recommend that you shut all internal doors and open external windows and doors to help with ventilation.

easy

Recipes are graded as follows:
1 spoon = easy;
2 spoons = very easy;
3 spoons = extremely easy.

serves 4

Recipes generally serve four people. Simply halve the ingredients to serve two, taking care not to mix metric and imperial measurements.

15 minutes

Preparation time. Where marinating or soaking are involved, these times have been added on separately: eg, 15 minutes + 30 minutes to marinate.

40 minutes

Cooking time. Cooking times do not include the cooking of side dishes or accompaniments served with the main dishes.

grilled pepper & courgette salad
page 64

fruit kebabs
page 74

Fish and griddling make an ideal combination, bringing out the flavour and texture of the fish to perfection. There is such a wide range of fresh or frozen fish available today that it should be possible to find something to please everyone. More than any other ingredient, however, fish must be as fresh as possible when prepared and eaten. The simple addition of lemon or lime juice and fresh herbs is usually quite sufficient, but vegetables can transform a basic dish into something quite exquisite.

fish & seafood

monkfish kebabs

very easy   serves 4

15 minutes   10–15
+ 1 hour to   minutes
marinate

ingredients

750 g/1 lb 10 oz monkfish, skinned
and boned

MARINADE
50 ml/2 fl oz vegetable oil,
plus extra for basting
1 tsp paprika

1 red onion, cut into 8 pieces
8 button mushrooms
1 red or green pepper, deseeded and cut
into 8 pieces
2 courgettes, cut into 8 thick slices

4 tomatoes, halved, to garnish

Cut the monkfish into bite-sized cubes. Place in a glass dish, pour over the oil and sprinkle with paprika. Mix well. Cover the dish with clingfilm and refrigerate for at least 1 hour.

Remove the monkfish from the refrigerator and bring back to room temperature. Select skewers that will fit on your griddle. Soak wooden skewers in water for 30 minutes to prevent burning. Preheat the griddle over a moderate heat.

Assemble the kebabs, threading pieces of fish alternated with the vegetable pieces. Place the kebabs on the griddle and cook for 10–15 minutes, turning frequently and basting occasionally with oil, or until the fish is firm and the vegetables tender. If you wish, place the tomato halves on the griddle for the last 2–3 minutes.

Serve the kebabs on individual serving plates, garnished with raw or cooked tomato halves.

whole grilled fish

easy   serves 4

10 minutes
+ 1 hour
to rest

10–15
minutes

ingredients

4 tbsp chopped fresh mint
4 tbsp chopped fresh parsley
4 tbsp chopped fresh tarragon
4 x 350 g/12 oz trout, herring or bass,
   cleaned and gutted
salt and pepper
juice of 1 lemon

4 tbsp butter, diced
1 tbsp oil or butter, for brushing

TO SERVE
new potatoes
green beans with almonds

Mix the herbs together in a small bowl. Place one quarter of the mixture in the cavity of each fish, reserving a small amount for serving. Gently press the fish closed.

Make two or three shallow cuts on each side of the fish. Sprinkle with salt, pepper and half of the lemon juice. Rub in well and leave to rest for 1 hour.

Preheat the griddle over a medium heat. Spray or brush with oil or melted butter.

Dot the fish with half of the diced butter, then place it, buttered side down, on the griddle. After about 6 minutes, when the bottom is brown and crispy, sprinkle the remaining lemon juice on top, dot with the remaining butter and turn to cook the second side.

Transfer the cooked fish to individual plates and serve with boiled new potatoes and green beans with almonds.

seafood brochettes

very easy   serves 4

5 minutes   10–15
minutes

ingredients

4 scallops, cleaned
4 baby squid, cleaned
4 tiger prawns, in their shells
4 button mushrooms
4 cherry tomatoes
4 baby sweetcorn cobs, optional
2 tbsp vegetable oil, for basting

a few sprigs of flat-leaved parsley,
    to garnish

buttered rice, to serve

Select skewers that will fit on your griddle. If using wooden skewers, soak them in water for 30 minutes to prevent burning. Preheat the griddle over a medium heat.

Meanwhile, assemble the kebabs, threading several pieces of all three types of seafood and the vegetables alternately on each.

Place the kebabs on the griddle and cook for 5–10 minutes, turning frequently and basting occasionally with oil, or until the fish is firm and the vegetables are tender. Be very careful not to overcook the squid (which will make it tough).

Remove the kebabs from the griddle and transfer to individual serving plates. Garnish with parsley and serve with buttered rice.

lime-basted tuna steaks

extremely easy   serves 4

5 minutes
+ 30 minutes
to marinate   5 minutes

4 x 125 g/4½ oz fresh tuna steaks,
  sliced thinly

MARINADE
juice of 1 lime
2 tbsp vegetable oil

mixed salad leaves, to serve

Arrange the tuna steaks in a single layer in a shallow dish.

To make the marinade, combine the lime juice and oil in a small bowl. Whisk well, then pour over the fish. Cover the dish with clingfilm and refrigerate for 30 minutes.

Preheat the griddle over a high heat. Remove the fish from the refrigerator and bring back to room temperature. Drain off the marinade and pat the fish dry with kitchen paper.

Place the tuna on the griddle and sear quickly, then turn and sear the second side. Reduce the heat to medium and cook for 3 minutes longer, or until the fish is firm but still pink inside.

Remove the fish from the griddle and serve immediately with mixed salad leaves.

lemon-grilled salmon

very easy   serves 4

5 minutes   10–15
             minutes

ingredients

900 g/2 lb salmon fillet, cut into
    four pieces
juice of 1 lemon

55 g/2 oz butter, diced
salt and pepper

fresh parsley or dill, to garnish

Preheat the griddle over a high heat.

Sprinkle the fish with lemon juice, dot with butter and season with salt and pepper.

Place the salmon on the hot griddle, skin side down. Cook for 10–15 minutes, turning once when the first side is brown and crusty. The exact cooking time will vary depending on the thickness of the fillet. When it is ready, the fish should be firm and flake easily with a fork.

Transfer the steaks to a serving dish and serve with sprigs of fresh herbs arranged around the fish to garnish.

caribbean lobster skewers

easy   serves 4

15 minutes   10–15 minutes

ingredients

2 cooked lobsters or lobster tails
1 small pineapple
1 red pepper, deseeded and cut into
   8 pieces
4 shallots, quartered
55 g/2 oz butter, melted

TO SERVE
sautéed potatoes
green salad

Select skewers that will fit on your griddle. If using wooden skewers, soak them in water for 30 minutes to prevent burning.

Remove the lobster meat from its shell, cut into large chunks and set aside. Skin the pineapple, then cut lengthways into quarters. Remove the hard core and cut each wedge into quarters.

Preheat the griddle over a moderate heat while you assemble the kebabs. Thread each skewer with several pieces of lobster alternated with pineapple, pepper and shallots. Brush the kebabs with the melted butter.

Cook on the griddle for 10–15 minutes, depending on the size of the pieces, or until the lobster is thoroughly heated and the vegetables tender. Turn frequently and baste occasionally.

Remove the kebabs from the griddle and transfer to individual serving plates. Serve with sautéed potatoes and a green salad.

king prawns with lemon & lime leaf

very easy   serves 4
             as a starter

5 minutes   10 minutes
+ 1 hour
to marinate

ingredients

12 large tiger prawns

MARINADE
2 spring onions, chopped finely
juice of ½ lemon
1 tsp fresh chopped lime leaf
1 tsp red chilli, deseeded and chopped
   finely or 1 tsp dried hot chilli flakes

TO SERVE
garlic mayonnaise
lemon wedges

Place the prawns in a large mixing bowl. Add the marinade ingredients and mix well. Cover the bowl with clingfilm and refrigerate for 1 hour.

Preheat the griddle over a high heat and remove the prawns from the refrigerator.

Cook the prawns for 2–3 minutes on each side, turning once and ensuring that the shells are crispy and well browned.

Transfer the prawns to a large serving dish. Serve immediately with a bowl of garlic mayonnaise and lemon wedges.

seared chilli mint scallops

very easy   serves 4

15 minutes   5 minutes
+ 30 minutes
to marinate

ingredients

16–24 scallops, detached from shells
  and cleaned

MARINADE
2 tbsp vegetable oil
2 tsp fish sauce
juice of ½ lime
1 garlic clove, crushed
1 small fresh chilli, deseeded and
  chopped finely

2 tbsp chopped fresh basil leaves
1 tbsp chopped fresh mint leaves
½ tsp chopped fresh lime leaf

TO SERVE
mixed salad leaves
2 tbsp olive oil and 1 tbsp lemon juice
  (mixed), for salad dressing
fresh croûtons or Tomato Basil Bruschetta
  (see page 58)

Place the scallops in a large glass dish. Combine all the marinade ingredients in a mixing bowl. Stir until they make a thick paste. Pour over the scallops and turn gently to coat. Cover the dish with clingfilm and refrigerate for at least 30 minutes.

Preheat the griddle over a high heat. Remove the scallops from the refrigerator and bring back to room temperature. Drain well and pat dry with kitchen paper.

Place the scallops on the griddle and cook over a high heat for 1–2 minutes, or until well seared. Turn and cook the second side for 1–2 minutes. Be careful not to overcook.

Remove the scallops and carefully arrange them on individual serving plates. Garnish with mixed salad leaves sprinkled with a simple olive oil and lemon juice dressing. Sprinkle with croûtons or serve with Tomato Basil Bruschetta.

tasty thai fish patties

easy   serves 4

10 minutes   5 minutes
+ 30 minutes
to chill

ingredients

1 kg/2 lb 4 oz cod, haddock, whiting or
  coley fillet (skinned), or a mixture
1 small onion
1 small fresh chilli,
  deseeded (optional)
6–8 tbsp fresh breadcrumbs
1 egg
2 tbsp fish sauce
juice of ½ lime
1 tbsp finely chopped fresh
  lemon grass

2 tsp finely grated fresh ginger
2 tsp chopped fresh coriander
pinch of sugar
pinch of salt

1–2 tbsp vegetable oil, for brushing

fresh coriander and lemon grass,
  to garnish

chilli sauce or sweet soy sauce, to serve

Cut the fish into large pieces, place in a food processor with the onion and chilli
(if using) and chop finely. Transfer the fish mixture to a mixing bowl and add all
the other recipe ingredients. Mix well. The mixture should be quite thick and stiff.

Cover the bowl with clingfilm and refrigerate for at least 30 minutes. Remove the
fish from the refrigerator and mix once more. Brush the griddle with oil and
preheat over a high heat.

Form small patties from the fish mixture, place on the griddle and cook in batches
for 3–4 minutes, or until golden, turning once. If necessary, brush the griddle with
another tablespoon of oil before cooking the next batch of patties.

Transfer the cooked patties to a serving dish and garnish with coriander leaves and
stalks of lemon grass. Serve warm or cold, accompanied by chilli sauce or sweet
soy sauce.

fennel-basted trout fillets

very easy   serves 4

10 minutes   10 minutes
+ 30 minutes
to marinate

ingredients

MARINADE
4 tsp vegetable oil
juice of ½ lemon
4 sprigs fresh fennel, chopped finely
salt and pepper

4 fresh trout, filleted

GARNISH
fennel sprigs
lemon wedges

To make the marinade, combine the oil and lemon juice in a small mixing bowl and whisk together. Stir in the chopped fennel, salt and pepper.

Place the trout fillets in a shallow glass dish. Pour over the fennel mixture, cover the dish with clingfilm and marinate in the refrigerator for 30 minutes.

Heat the griddle over a medium heat. Remove the trout from the refrigerator and bring back to room temperature for 10 minutes. Transfer the trout to the griddle and brush any remaining marinade over the fish. Cook the fillets for about 5 minutes on each side, turning once and brushing with the marinade.

Remove the trout from the griddle and arrange on an attractive serving dish. Serve at once, garnished with sprigs of fennel and lemon wedges.

nut-crusted halibut

extremely
easy

serves 4

5 minutes

10 minutes

ingredients

3 tbsp butter, melted

750 g/1 lb 10 oz halibut fillet

55 g/2 oz pistachio nuts, shelled
and chopped very finely

Brush the melted butter over the fish fillet.

Roll the fish in the chopped nuts, pressing down gently.

Preheat the griddle. Cook the halibut over a medium heat for approximately
10 minutes, turning once. Cooking time will depend on the thickness of the fillet,
but the fish should be firm and tender when done.

Remove the fish and any loose pistachio pieces from the heat and transfer to
a large serving platter. Serve immediately.

Griddling meat is as close to indoor barbecuing as it gets. The charred appearance and smoky flavour are almost as good when meat is seared on a griddle as over charcoal. These dishes are incredibly quick and easy and also offer great flexibility in terms of marinades, sauces and accompaniments. What more can you ask for at the end of a busy day?

meat & poultry

spatchcocked poussin

easy   serves 4

5 minutes   40 minutes

ingredients

2 poussins
4 tbsp extra virgin olive oil
4 sprigs fresh rosemary
2 small fresh chilli peppers, deseeded and
    diced (optional)
coarsely ground sea salt

2 sprigs of rosemary, to garnish

mixed salad, to serve

To spatchcock the poussins, cut through the backbone with a very sharp knife or poultry shears, then turn the bird breast side up on a chopping board and press hard to flatten. Do not cut all the way through. Preheat the griddle over a high heat.

Place the poussin, skin side up, on the griddle. Brush with oil and arrange a sprig of rosemary on each of the four sections. Scatter over chilli peppers (if using) and sea salt.

Cook the poussins for 10 minutes, or until the underside is seared. Turn and sear the skin side, then reduce the heat to medium. Continue cooking for 30 minutes longer, or until the juices in the leg run clear when pierced with a skewer.

Transfer the poussin to a chopping board, cut the bone through so that you have four halves, then arrange on an attractive serving dish, garnished with more rosemary. Serve with a mixed salad.

lemon & thyme chicken portions

very easy   serves 4

10 minutes   35–40
+ 4–6 hours minutes
to marinate

ingredients

4 chicken portions
salt and pepper

MARINADE
1 garlic clove, crushed
8 sprigs of fresh thyme, finely chopped
juice and grated rind of 1 lemon
4 tbsp olive oil

GARNISH
lemon wedges
sprigs of thyme

Arrange the chicken portions in a single layer in a shallow dish. Season to taste with salt and pepper.

Mix the marinade ingredients in a small bowl, then spoon over the chicken. Cover with clingfilm and marinate in the refrigerator for 4–6 hours or overnight. Turn the portions occasionally.

Before cooking the chicken, allow it to return to room temperature. Preheat the griddle over a high heat.

Place the chicken on the griddle skin side down, and cook for 10 minutes, or until the skin is crisp and starting to brown. Turn, and brown the underside, pressing down occasionally. Reduce the heat to medium and cook for a further 20 minutes, or until the juices of leg pieces run clear when pierced with a skewer.

Remove the chicken, place on a warm serving dish and serve garnished with lemon wedges and sprigs of thyme.

italian lamb chops

very easy   serves 4

5 minutes   10 minutes
+ 8–12
hours to
marinate

4 lamb chops or 8 lamb cutlets
4 tomatoes, halved

MARINADE
2 tsp dried oregano
juice of ½ lemon
2 tbsp extra virgin olive oil
a few basil leaves, to garnish

cooked linguine or other pasta, to serve

Arrange the lamb in a single layer in a shallow dish. Sprinkle with oregano, lemon juice and oil. Cover the dish with clingfilm and refrigerate overnight or for as long as possible.

About 10 minutes before cooking, remove the lamb from the refrigerator. Meanwhile, preheat the griddle over a high heat.

Place the lamb on the griddle and sear for 2 minutes on each side. Reduce the heat and cook over a medium heat for about 5 minutes longer, turning the pieces over once. If the chops are thick, you may need to allow a few extra minutes. The meat is best when it is pink inside.

Two to three minutes before the meat is ready, cook the tomato pieces on the griddle. Arrange the chops and cooked tomatoes on a large platter and serve immediately with the pasta (if using), garnished with basil leaves.

coriander lamb kebabs

very easy   serves 4

20 minutes   15 minutes
+ 8–12
hours to
marinate

MARINADE
1 bunch fresh coriander, torn
1 large onion, quartered

KEBABS
750 g/1 lb 10 oz boneless lamb, cubed
1 red onion, quartered
2 courgettes, quartered
8 cherry or baby plum tomatoes

Set aside 2 tablespoons of coriander leaves.

Blend the onion and remaining coriander in a food processor until you have a coarse, slushy mixture. Transfer to a large mixing bowl, add the lamb and toss to coat. Cover the bowl with clingfilm and refrigerate overnight.

Select skewers that comfortably fit your griddle. If using wooden sticks, soak them in water for 30 minutes.

Remove the lamb from the refrigerator and stir again. Preheat the griddle over a high heat. Thread the lamb onto the skewers, alternating with the vegetable pieces. Cook for 5 minutes, then reduce the heat to medium and cook for a further 10 minutes, or until the vegetables start to soften and the meat is cooked but still pink. Turn frequently and brush with any remaining marinade.

Serve the kebabs garnished with the reserved coriander leaves.

middle eastern koftas

very easy   serves 4

10 minutes   10 minutes

ingredients

750 g/1 lb 10 oz minced lamb or beef
1 small onion, quartered
2 garlic cloves, crushed
2 tbsp chopped fresh flat-leaved parsley
1 tsp coriander seeds
½ tsp cumin seeds
½ tsp whole black peppercorns
generous pinch of ground cinnamon

pinch of salt
Minted Yogurt Marinade (see page 94)
fresh mint and lemon wedges, to garnish

SERVING SUGGESTIONS

rice or Indian bread
cucumber yogurt raita
tomato and onion salad

Blend the meat, onion, garlic, parsley, spices and seasoning to a smooth paste in a food processor. Turn into a large mixing bowl.

Select flat skewers that fit comfortably onto your griddle.

Take about 2 tablespoons of meat paste and roll gently between your palms to make a sausage shape. Carefully fold around the skewer. If you cannot find flat skewers, shape the meat into patties as you would for hamburgers.

Preheat the griddle over a high heat. Brush the koftas with minted yoghurt marinade and cook for 10 minutes, turning carefully and basting regularly.

When the meat is cooked, transfer to a large serving platter and garnish with sprigs of fresh mint and lemon wedges. Serve with rice or Indian bread and bowls of cucumber yogurt raita and tomato onion salad.

homestyle hamburgers

easy   serves 4

5 minutes   10 minutes

750 g/1 lb 10 oz minced beef
1 beef stock cube
1 tbsp minced dried onion
2 tbsp water
55 g/2 oz grated Cheddar cheese, optional

SERVING SUGGESTIONS
4 sesame buns
tomato ketchup or chilli sauce
mustard
pickled cucumbers, sliced thinly
Spanish onion, sliced thinly
large tomato, sliced thinly
lettuce leaves
chips

Place the beef in a large mixing bowl. Crumble the stock cube over the meat, add the dried onion and water and mix well. Divide the meat into four portions, shape each into a ball, then flatten slightly to make a burger shape of your preferred thickness.

Preheat the griddle over a high heat. Place the burgers on the griddle and cook for about 5 minutes on each side, depending on how well done you like your meat and the thickness of the burgers. Press down occasionally with a flat turner or palette knife during cooking.

To make cheeseburgers, sprinkle the cheese on top of the meat when you have turned it the first time.

Serve the burgers on toasted buns, with a selection of the accompaniments suggested above.

corned beef hash

very easy   serves 4

5 minutes   20–25 minutes

ingredients

55 g/2 oz butter
1 small onion, chopped finely
1 medium cooked potato, diced
350g/12 oz canned corned beef, diced

salad, to serve

Melt the butter over a medium heat in a small frying pan. Add the onion and cook for 5 minutes to soften. Stir in the potatoes and corned beef and mix well.

Preheat the griddle over a medium heat. Turn the corned beef mixture onto the griddle and press together firmly to make one large patty or four small ones. Cook for 5–8 minutes, or until the underside is well browned, then turn and cook the other side in the same way, making sure that the corned beef is thoroughly heated through.

Lift the hash onto individual serving plates and serve with salad.

sticky pork steaks

very easy   serves 4

5 minutes   10–15
minutes

SAUCE

50 ml/2 fl oz plum, hoisin, sweet & sour
 or duck sauce

1 tsp dark brown sugar

1 tbsp tomato ketchup

pinch of garlic powder

2 tbsp dark soy sauce

4 lean pork steaks

cooked rice and peas, to serve

Preheat the griddle over a high heat.

Combine the sauce, brown sugar, ketchup, garlic powder and soy sauce in a
small mixing bowl.

Arrange the pork steaks in a single layer on a flat dish. Brush the tops with
sauce, then place the steaks, sauce side down, on the griddle. Cook the steaks
for 5 minutes, pressing down occasionally to get dark grid marks.

Brush the upper side of the steaks with sauce, turn and continue cooking for
5 minutes, or until dark grid marks appear.

Reduce the heat to medium and, turning once, cook the steaks for about
10 more minutes, or until they are firm and the juices run clear when pierced
with a skewer.

Transfer the steaks to a large dish and serve immediately, with the peas and rice.

sweet & sour pork kebabs

very easy   serves 4

15 minutes   15 minutes
+ 1 hour
to marinate

ingredients

450 g/1 lb boneless pork, cubed
Sweet & Sour Marinade (see page 92)
2 carrots, peeled and sliced thickly
1 small red pepper, deseeded and quartered
1 small green pepper, deseeded and
    quartered
2 tomatoes, halved
1 onion, peeled and quartered

SAUCE
2 tbsp cornflour
2 tsp sugar
1 tbsp wine vinegar
2 tbsp sweet sherry
600 ml/1 pint water
3 tbsp tomato purée
8 knobs stem ginger, diced
2 tbsp ginger syrup

Mix the pork in a bowl with the marinade. Cover with clingfilm and refrigerate for 1 hour, stirring occasionally. Blanch the carrots for 5 minutes in a pan of boiling water. Drain and cool.

Remove the meat from the refrigerator and stir. Drain from the marinade. Heat the griddle over a medium heat. Thread the meat and vegetables on skewers, then, turning frequently, cook the kebabs on the griddle for 10–15 minutes, or until tender.

To make the sauce, mix the cornflour and sugar in a small pan. Add the vinegar and sherry, stirring to eliminate lumps. Gradually add the water and tomato purée, still stirring. Mix in the ginger pieces and syrup. Cook over a medium heat, stirring constantly, until it comes to the boil and thickens slightly.

Remove the kebabs and serve drizzled with a spoonful of sauce.

satay sticks

very easy · serves 4

15 minutes
+ 1 hour
to marinate

25 minutes

ingredients

4 chicken breasts, skinned and boned,
   or 4 boneless pork steaks

MARINADE
2 tbsp finely chopped onion
1 garlic clove, chopped finely
2 tbsp chopped fresh coriander
2 tbsp soy sauce
¼ tsp ground ginger
¼ tsp sugar
1 tbsp vegetable oil

PEANUT SAUCE
1 small onion, chopped finely
2 garlic cloves
1 red chilli pepper, deseeded and minced
1 tbsp light brown sugar
1 tbsp vegetable oil
125 g/4½ oz crunchy peanut butter
1 tbsp lemon or lime juice
1 tbsp dark soy sauce
400 ml/14 fl oz coconut milk

rice and fresh coriander, to serve

Cut the meat into thin slices, about 5 cm/2 inches long. Combine the marinade ingredients in a shallow dish. Add the meat and stir well. Cover with clingfilm and refrigerate for 1 hour or more.

For the sauce, blend the onion, garlic, chilli and sugar into a coarse paste in a food processor. Cook in the oil in a small pan over a medium heat for 5 minutes. Add the remaining sauce ingredients and mix well. Bring to the boil, then simmer and cook until thickened slightly (about 15 minutes), stirring constantly.

Preheat the griddle over a high heat. Drain the meat and thread onto skewers. Brush with oil and cook on the griddle for 3–4 minutes on each side, or until the meat is cooked through.

Serve the satay sticks on a bed of rice with fresh coriander. Put the peanut sauce in a small serving dish as an accompaniment.

seared duck breast

very easy   serves 4

5 minutes   25 minutes

ingredients

4 boneless duck breasts

4 tbsp honey

2 tbsp orange juice

2 tsp soy sauce

TO SERVE

boiled potatoes

salad

Score across the skin of the duck breast diagonally at intervals of 2.5 cm/1 inch.

Preheat the griddle over a high heat. Place the duck on the griddle, skin side down, and cook for 5 minutes, or until it is starting to brown. Turn, reduce the heat to medium and cook for an additional 10–15 minutes.

While the duck is cooking, combine the honey, orange juice and soy sauce.

Turn the duck so that it is skin side up, spoon over the sauce and cook for another 5 minutes.

Transfer the breasts to a carving board and slice thinly at an angle. Arrange the slices on a serving dish. Serve at once, with boiled potatoes or other vegetables of your choice and salad.

glazed gammon steaks

easy   serves 4

5 minutes   10 minutes

ingredients

4 gammon steaks
4 tbsp dark brown sugar
2 tsp mustard powder
4 tbsp butter
8 slices pineapple

TO SERVE
baked potato
green beans

Preheat the griddle over a medium heat, place the gammon steaks on it and cook for 5 minutes, turning once. If you have room for only two steaks at a time, cook them completely and keep warm while cooking the second pair.

Combine the brown sugar and mustard in a small bowl.

Melt the butter in a large frying pan, add the pineapple and cook for 2 minutes to heat through, turning once. Sprinkle with the sugar and mustard and continue cooking over a low heat until the sugar has melted and the pineapple is well glazed. Turn the pineapple once more so that both sides are coated with sauce.

Place the gammon steaks on individual plates and arrange 2 pineapple slices either next to them or overlapping on top. Spoon over some of the sweet pan juices.

Serve with a baked potato and green beans.

Whatever meal you are planning can be enhanced by serving griddled vegetables, such as Crunchy Griddled Asparagus, either as a starter or an accompaniment to the main course. Vegetables should be dressed or marinated after cooking, rather than before, because they are less absorbent when raw. A simple dressing of either melted butter, oil and lemon or lime juice, or just a dash of balsamic vinegar, add zing to your selection of vegetables.

vegetables

tomato basil bruschetta

extremely easy serves 4

10 minutes 5 minutes

ingredients

1 small oval-shaped loaf of white bread (ciabatta or bloomer)
125 ml/4 fl oz extra virgin olive oil
4 tomatoes
6 leaves fresh basil

salt and pepper
8 black olives, stoned and chopped (optional)
1 large garlic clove

Cut the bread into 1 cm/½ inch slices. Pour half of the oil into a shallow dish and place the bread in it. Leave for 2–3 minutes, turn and leave for 2 more minutes, or until thoroughly saturated in oil.

Meanwhile, deseed and dice the tomatoes and place in a mixing bowl. Tear the basil leaves and sprinkle over the tomatoes. Season with salt and pepper. Add the olives, if using. Pour over the remaining olive oil and leave to marinate.

Preheat the griddle over a medium heat. Cook the bread until golden and crispy on both sides (about 2 minutes on each side). Remove the bread from the griddle and arrange on an attractive serving dish.

Peel the garlic clove and cut in half. Rub the cut edges over the surface of the bruschetta. Top each slice with a spoonful of the tomato mixture and serve.

vegetable kebabs

very easy   serves 4

10 minutes   10 minutes

ingredients

4 cherry or baby plum tomatoes

2 courgettes, quartered

8 button mushrooms

4 shallots, whole, peeled

2 red or green peppers, deseeded and
 quartered

4 tbsp olive oil

salt and pepper

mixed salad leaves, to serve

2 tbsp chopped fresh basil or oregano,
 to garnish

Select skewers that will fit comfortably on your griddle. Pre-soak wooden
skewers in water for 30 minutes, if using.

Preheat the griddle over a high heat.

Meanwhile, arrange all the vegetables on the skewers, alternating to create
a colourful selection. Brush with olive oil and season with salt and pepper.

Place the kebabs on the griddle and cook, turning frequently, for about 10 minutes.
Baste with olive oil occasionally, so that the vegetables don't dry out.

Remove the kebabs from the griddle, arrange on a serving platter and serve
with the mixed salad leaves, garnished with the chopped herbs.

grilled aubergine pâté

very easy   serves 4

10 minutes   10 minutes

2 small aubergines
2 tbsp olive oil
juice of 1 lemon
4 tbsp tahini
2 garlic cloves, crushed (optional)

TO SERVE
carrot sticks
celery sticks
hot pitta bread

Preheat the griddle over a high heat. Place the aubergines on the griddle. Turning frequently, cook for about 10 minutes, or until the skins are black and blistered and the aubergines are very soft.

Remove the aubergines from the griddle and cool slightly. Cut in half and scoop out the insides into a mixing bowl. Mash with a fork to make a coarse paste.

Gradually add the olive oil, lemon juice and tahini. Stir in the garlic, if using. Mix well, tasting and adjusting ingredient amounts, until you achieve the flavour and texture you like.

Transfer the mixture to an attractive bowl and serve with sticks of raw carrots and celery and hot pitta bread.

grilled pepper & courgette salad

easy   serves 4

10 minutes   20 minutes
+ 3–4 hours
to marinate

ingredients

1 red pepper, halved, cored and
deseeded

1 green pepper, halved, cored and
deseeded

1 yellow pepper, halved, cored and
deseeded

2 courgettes, quartered lengthways

2 tbsp olive oil, to brush

DRESSING

2 tbsp balsamic vinegar

4 tbsp olive oil

2 tsp fresh chopped oregano

salt and pepper

115 g/4 oz feta cheese (drained weight),
cubed (optional), to serve

Preheat the griddle over a high heat. Cook the peppers on the griddle until the
skins are blackened and the flesh is soft (about 2 minutes each side). Remove
from the griddle and wrap in damp kitchen paper until cool enough to handle.

Brush the courgette pieces with oil, place on the hot griddle and cook until soft
and well browned on both sides (about 2 minutes each side). Remove and place
in a large shallow serving dish.

Remove the kitchen paper from the peppers and peel off the skins. Cut each piece
into four strips and add to the courgettes. Sprinkle the vinegar and olive oil over
the vegetables and mix well. Toss with the oregano. Season to taste.

Cover with clingfilm and leave in a cool place, or in the refrigerator, for 3–4 hours.
Before serving, stir through once and add the feta cheese, if using. Serve the salad
at room temperature.

buttery rosemary potatoes

very easy   serves 4

10 minutes   25 minutes

ingredients

16 small new potatoes

55 g/2 oz butter

2 tbsp fresh rosemary, chopped finely

salt and pepper

Cook the potatoes in boiling salted water for 12–15 minutes, or until just tender. Drain well and gently rub off the skins.

Melt the butter in a large pan along with the rosemary, reserving a little rosemary to garnish.

Preheat the griddle over a medium heat.

Toss the potatoes in the melted butter until well coated. Transfer to the griddle and cook until golden on all sides (5–10 minutes), turning often and basting with the rosemary butter.

Arrange the potatoes in a serving dish, sprinkle generously with salt and pepper and serve garnished with the reserved rosemary.

crispy sweet & white potatoes

easy   serves 4

5 minutes   20 minutes

450 g/1 lb waxy white potatoes
450 g/1 lb sweet potatoes (yams)
125 g/4½ oz butter, melted
salt and pepper

TO SERVE
salad leaves
dips or salsas

Preheat the griddle over a medium heat.

Thinly slice the potatoes. Brush with melted butter, then place them on the griddle in batches and cook for 5–10 minutes, turning once, until brown and crispy.

Transfer the first batch of cooked potatoes to a serving dish and keep warm while cooking the remainder.

Sprinkle generously with salt and pepper before serving with salad leaves as an accompaniment to a fish or meat main meal, or with your favourite dips or salsas as a starter or as a snack with drinks.

crunchy griddled asparagus

very easy   serves 4

5 minutes   5–10
              minutes

ingredients

450 g/1 lb asparagus spears, all of similar
   thickness
2 tbsp extra virgin olive oil
1 tsp coarse sea salt
juice of ½ lemon
black pepper

25 g/1 oz thinly shaved Parmesan cheese
   (optional)

Preheat the griddle over a medium heat.

Trim the base of the asparagus spears so that they are approximately the
same length.

Arrange the asparagus in a single layer on the griddle. Drizzle with olive oil
and sprinkle with the salt. Cook for 5–10 minutes, turning frequently. Asparagus
is particularly tasty if it gets slightly crispy as well as charred. Remove from the
griddle and transfer to an attractive serving dish.

Sprinkle the lemon juice and black pepper over the asparagus. Serve topped with
Parmesan shavings, if using.

Hot griddled fruit is a special treat that is both juicy and crunchy at the same time. A coating of crispy browned sugar will seal in the flavour and texture of the fruit. Contrasting griddled fruit with a cold, creamy accompaniment makes the perfect end to a wonderful meal. From mouthwatering Fruit Kebabs to the sheer self-indulgence of Rum Bananas, the griddled desserts described in the following pages are deliciously tempting.

desserts

fruit kebabs

very easy   serves 4

10 minutes   10 minutes

ingredients

450 g/1 lb assorted fruit (peaches, apricots,
    plums, apples, pears)
55 g/2 oz butter, melted
2 tbsp sugar
pinch of cinnamon, optional

SERVING SUGGESTIONS
crème fraîche
natural yogurt
ice cream

Select skewers that will fit comfortably on your griddle. Pre-soak wooden skewers in water for 30 minutes, if using.

Preheat the griddle over a medium heat.

Stone the fruit as necessary, or remove cores, and cut into similar-sized pieces. Small fruit may be left whole. Arrange alternating pieces on the skewers. Brush the fruit with melted butter.

Spread the sugar on a plate large enough to take the skewers. Mix in the cinnamon, if using. Roll the fruit kebabs in the sugar, pressing gently to coat.

Cook the kebabs on the griddle, turning occasionally. Cook for about 10 minutes, or until the sugar has melted and started to bubble. The fruit should still be firm.

Serve hot, with crème fraîche, natural yogurt or ice cream.

rum bananas

very easy   serves 4

1 minute   5–10
minutes

ingredients

4 bananas
4 tsp rum or Cointreau

SERVING SUGGESTIONS
sorbet
ice cream
double cream
crème fraîche

Preheat the griddle over a high heat.

Place the bananas, still in their skins, on the griddle. Cook for 5–10 minutes, or until the skins are black, turning occasionally.

Remove the bananas from the griddle, peel and place in individual serving bowls. Pour 1 teaspoonful of rum or Cointreau over each banana and serve while still hot, with a scoop of sorbet, ice cream, double cream or crème fraîche.

glazed pineapple slices

very easy   serves 4

5 minutes   5 minutes

ingredients

1 pineapple
50 ml/2 fl oz honey
115 g/4 oz butter, melted

SERVING SUGGESTION
fruit sorbet
crème fraîche
whipped cream
ice cream

mint leaves, to decorate

Peel and core the pineapple. Cut into thick slices, about 2.5 cm/1 inch wide.

Preheat the griddle over a medium heat. Meanwhile, heat the honey in a small pan over a medium heat, or in a bowl in the microwave, until it is liquid.

Brush both sides of the pineapple slices with the melted butter. Place on the griddle and cook for 2 minutes on each side, brushing with honey before and after turning so that both sides are well coated and sticky.

Remove the hot pineapple from the griddle. Decorate with mint leaves and serve with a scoop of fruit sorbet, crème fraîche, whipped cream or ice cream.

crunchy ginger apples

very easy   serves 4

5 minutes   10 minutes

ingredients

4 crisp, tart apples
2 tbsp lemon juice
2 tbsp butter, melted
2 tbsp demerara sugar
4 tbsp diced stem ginger

SERVING SUGGESTIONS
crème fraîche
whipped cream
ice cream

mint leaves, to decorate

Cut the apples in half through their circumference. Carefully remove the pips and core.

Place the lemon juice, butter and demerara sugar in three separate small dishes. Dip the cut side of the apples first in the lemon juice, then in the melted butter and, finally, in the sugar.

Preheat the griddle over a medium heat. Add the apples, cut side down, and cook for 5 minutes or until the sugar caramelises and the apple surfaces are dark. Turn and cook for an additional 5 minutes to blacken the skin. The cooked apples should still retain their crunch.

Arrange the apple halves in individual dishes (allowing two halves per serving), cut side up, and spoon diced ginger over each half. Decorate with mint leaves and serve with a bowl of crème fraîche, whipped cream or ice cream.

Sweet, spicy or herby sauces and marinades can make an enormous difference to simple griddle-cooked dishes. Marinating in advance in Honey Mustard Marinade, for example, allows the flavour of herbs or spices to be absorbed before cooking. Serving a complementary dressing or sauce, such as Plum Salsa, can highlight the taste of the quickly cooked main ingredients. The flavour of the marinade or the taste and texture of the sauce should enhance the main ingredient, without distracting from it.

sauces & marinades

plum salsa

very easy | serves 4 as side dish

15 minutes | none

ingredients

8 plums, stoned

4 tbsp red onion, chopped finely

1 medium bunch fresh coriander, chopped finely

2 small fresh chillis, deseeded and chopped finely

pinch of sugar

pinch of salt

Cut the plums into bite-sized chunks. Place in a large mixing bowl.

Add the onion, coriander, chillis and seasoning, mix well and serve immediately. This salsa is at its best when freshly made.

minted melon salsa

easy

serves 4 as
side dish

15 minutes

ingredients

175 g/6 oz cantaloupe, charentais or
  galia melon

115 g/4 oz cucumber
large handful of fresh mint, finely chopped

Cut the flesh of the melon from its shell and remove all the seeds. Cut into tiny dice. Place in a large mixing bowl.

Cut the cucumber in quarters lengthways and scrape away any seeds. Cut the flesh into tiny dice.

Add the cucumber to the melon with the mint and mix well. Leave to rest for 10 minutes before using.

Serve with griddled fish or poultry.

tomato coriander salsa

very easy

serves 4 as
a side dish

10 minutes

no cooking;
30 minutes
resting

450 g/1 lb ripe tomatoes, deseeded and
    quartered
4 tbsp olive oil
2 tbsp red wine vinegar
2 tbsp fresh chives, chopped finely
1 medium bunch fresh rocket or sorrel,
    chopped finely

1 medium bunch of fresh coriander,
    chopped finely
pinch of sugar
salt and pepper

Cut the tomato quarters into strips and place them in a large mixing bowl.

Add the oil and vinegar to the tomatoes and mix well.

Add the chives, rocket (or sorrel, if using) and coriander, then season to taste with
sugar, salt and pepper and mix well. Leave to rest for 30 minutes before serving.

honey mustard marinade

easy   serves 4

5 minutes   none

ingredients

2 tbsp honey

2 tbsp wholegrain mustard

1 tsp ground ginger

1 tsp garlic powder

2 tsp fresh rosemary, chopped finely

4 tbsp dark soy sauce

50 ml/2 fl oz olive oil

Combine all the ingredients except the oil in a small mixing bowl.

Gradually add the oil, whisking constantly, until it is fully absorbed into the mixture.

Use to marinate and baste chicken or pork, especially spare ribs.

sweet & sour marinade

extremely easy   serves 4

5 minutes   none

225 ml/8 fl oz orange, grapefruit or
   pineapple juice
2 tbsp sweet sherry
125 ml/4 fl oz dark soy sauce
125 ml/4 fl oz chicken stock

50 ml/2 fl oz cider vinegar
1 tbsp tomato purée
55 g/2 oz light brown sugar
1 tsp powdered garlic
1 tsp powdered ginger

Combine the fruit juice, sherry, soy sauce, chicken stock and cider vinegar
in a mixing bowl.

Stir in the tomato purée, sugar, garlic and ginger. Mix well.

This mixture can be used to marinate and baste chicken or pork.

minted yogurt marinade

extremely easy

serves 4

10 minutes

2 garlic cloves, crushed
1 tsp salt
4 tbsp finely chopped fresh mint
225 ml/8 fl oz plain yogurt

1 tsp ground cumin, coriander seeds
   or cinnamon, optional
1 onion, optional

Mix the garlic with the salt to make a paste. Turn into a mixing bowl and stir in the mint, yogurt and cumin (or coriander or cinnamon, if using).

If you are using onion, place it in a food processor together with the yogurt mixture and blend for a few seconds, or until the mixture is coarse and the onions blended in.

Use to marinate and baste lamb.

index